AMAZING
ORIGAMI

DINOSAUR WORLD

Gareth Stevens
PUBLISHING

Joe Fullman

Please visit our website, **www.garethstevens.com**.
For a free color catalog of all our high-quality books,
call toll free 1-800-542-2595 or fax 1-877-542-2596.

Cataloging-in-Publication Data
Names: Fullman, Joe.
Title: Dinosaur world / Joe Fullman.
Description: New York : Gareth Stevens Publishing, 2019. | Series: Amazing origami | Includes glossary and index.
Identifiers: ISBN 9781538234723 (pbk.) | ISBN 9781538234747 (library bound) | ISBN 9781538234730 (6pack)
Subjects: LCSH: Origami--Juvenile literature. | Dinosaurs in art--Juvenile literature.
Classification: LCC TT872.5 F85 2019 | DDC 736'.982--dc23

First Edition

Published in 2019 by
Gareth Stevens Publishing
111 East 14th Street, Suite 349
New York, NY 10003

Copyright © Arcturus Holdings Ltd, 2019

Models created by Picnic
Photography by Michael Wilkes
Text by Joe Fullman
Design by Emma Randall

Printed in the United States of America

CPSIA compliance information: Batch #CW19GS: For further information contact Gareth Stevens, New York, New York at 1-800-542-2595.

CONTENTS

INTRODUCTION

Get ready for some fearsome folding as we explore the world of dinosaur origami. You'll learn how to create your own dinosaur world, from an eerie Jurassic eye to foreboding dino footprints.

A lot of the origami models in this book are made with the same folds and basic designs, known as "bases." This introduction explains some of the ones that will appear most, so it's a good idea to master those folds and bases before you start. When making the projects, follow the key below to find out what the lines and arrows mean.

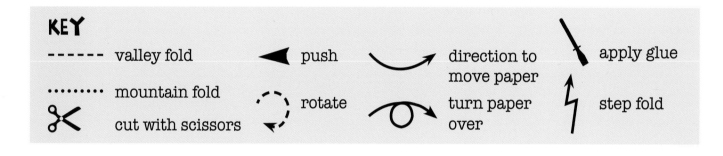

KEY

- – – – – valley fold
- ·········· mountain fold
- ✂ cut with scissors
- ◀ push
- ⟲ rotate
- ⤳ direction to move paper
- ⟳ turn paper over
- ⟋ apply glue
- ⚡ step fold

VALLEY FOLD

To make a valley fold, fold the paper toward you, so that the crease is pointing away from you, like a valley.

MOUNTAIN FOLD

To make a mountain fold, fold the paper so that the crease is pointing up toward you, like a mountain.

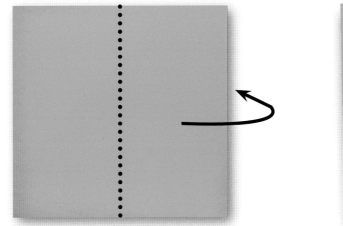 

STEP FOLD

A step fold is used to make a zigzag in the paper. We'll use it to make ears, tails, and other dino features.

1 Valley fold the paper in half. Then make a mountain fold directly above the valley fold.

2 Push the mountain fold down over the valley fold and press down flat.

3 You now have a step fold. You can also make it in reverse, with the mountain fold first.

This is a useful fold if you want to flatten part of an origami model. It's a good way to create tails and snouts for your dinosaurs.

 Fold a piece of paper diagonally in half. Make a valley fold on one corner and crease.

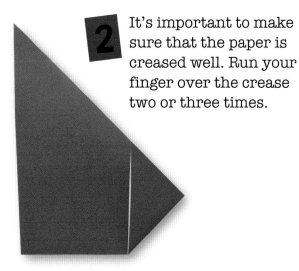 It's important to make sure that the paper is creased well. Run your finger over the crease two or three times.

 Refold the crease you just made into a mountain fold, then unfold. Open up the corner slightly.

 Open up the paper a little more and then tuck the tip of the corner inside. Close the paper. This is the view from the underside of the paper.

Flatten the paper. You now have an inside reverse fold.

This is great if you want to make part of your model stick out. It will come in handy for making heads and crests.

1 Fold a piece of paper diagonally in half. Make a valley fold on one corner and crease.

2 It's important to make sure that the paper is creased well. Run your finger over the crease two or three times.

3 Refold the crease you just made into a mountain fold, then unfold. Open up the corner slightly.

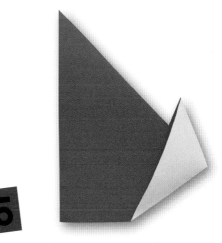

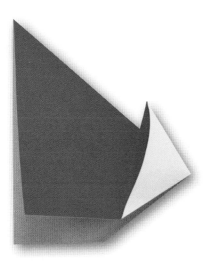

4 Open up the paper a little more and start to turn the corner inside out. Then close the paper when the fold begins to turn.

5 You now have an outside reverse fold. You can either flatten the paper or leave it rounded out.

KITE BASE

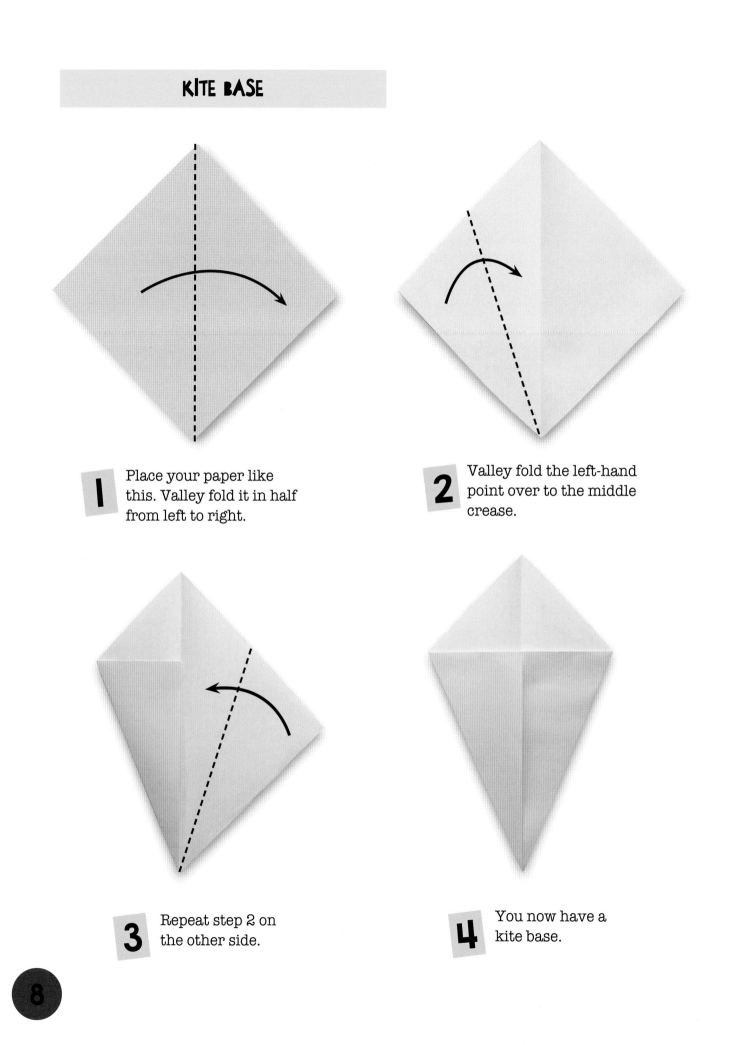

1 Place your paper like this. Valley fold it in half from left to right.

2 Valley fold the left-hand point over to the middle crease.

3 Repeat step 2 on the other side.

4 You now have a kite base.

DINO CLAWS

If you've ever wondered what it would be like to be a dinosaur, then this is the project for you. You'll need ten pieces of paper to make the full set of claws.

START WITH A KITE BASE

180°

1
Let's start with the first claw. Begin by making a kite base (see page 8), then rotate the paper 180°.

2

Fold the paper in half from left to right.

3
Fold the bottom point up and to the right.

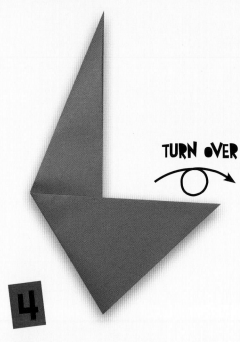

TURN OVER

4

Turn your paper over from right to left.

5

Fold the left-hand point over to the right.

TURN OVER

6

Turn the paper over again from right to left

7

Fold the left-hand point up and to the right along the fold line you made in step 3.

8

Now mountain fold the point over, tucking it behind the second layer of paper.

← OPEN

9

Open the paper up at the top on the right-hand side.

90°

10

Your paper should look like this. Rotate it 90° to the right.

11

To put on your first claw, insert your finger into the opening you made in step 9 and push it into the paper.

INSERT FINGER

12

Repeat all the steps nine more times and you'll have a full set of claws!

FINISHED!

JURASSIC EYE

Follow the steps to find out what it's like to stare a dinosaur right in the eye. Let's see who blinks first!

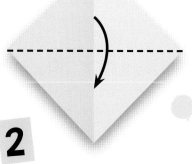

1
Place your paper like this, white side up, with a corner facing you. Fold in half from right to left, then unfold.

2
Now fold it in half from top to bottom and unfold.

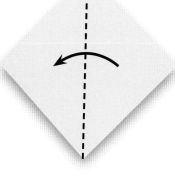

3
Fold the top point down to the central crease.

4
Fold the bottom point up to the central crease.

5
Fold the top edge down to the central crease.

6
Fold the bottom edge up to the central crease.

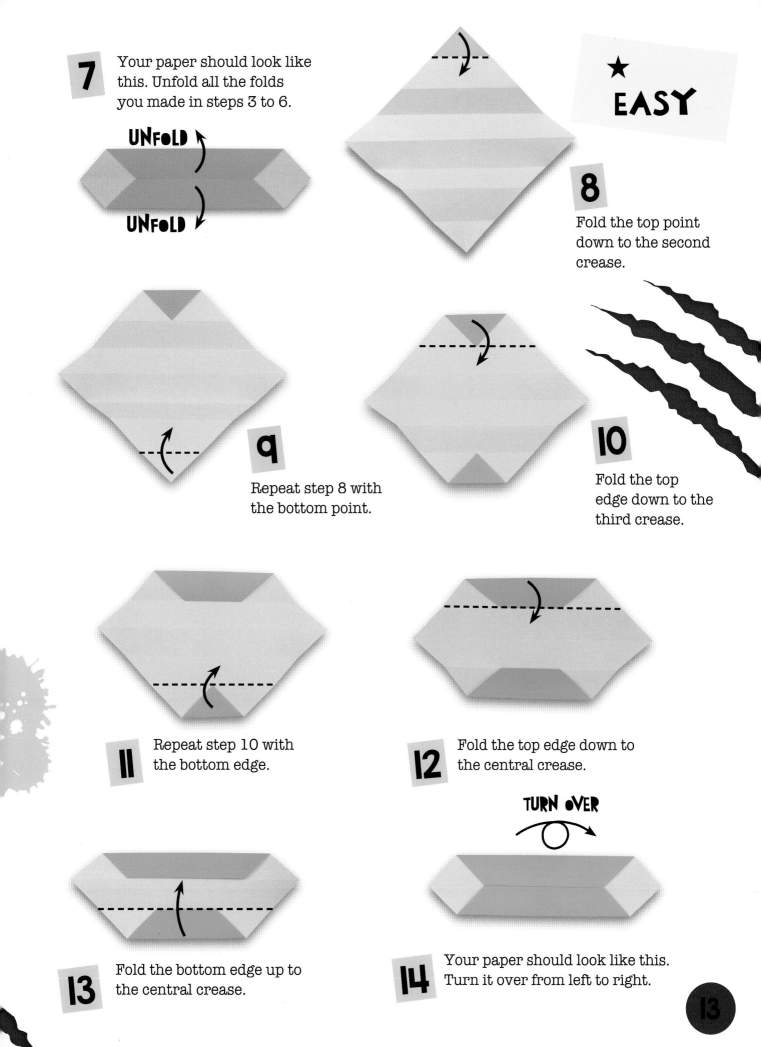

7 Your paper should look like this. Unfold all the folds you made in steps 3 to 6.

UNFOLD

UNFOLD

★ EASY

8 Fold the top point down to the second crease.

9 Repeat step 8 with the bottom point.

10 Fold the top edge down to the third crease.

11 Repeat step 10 with the bottom edge.

12 Fold the top edge down to the central crease.

TURN OVER

13 Fold the bottom edge up to the central crease.

14 Your paper should look like this. Turn it over from left to right.

13

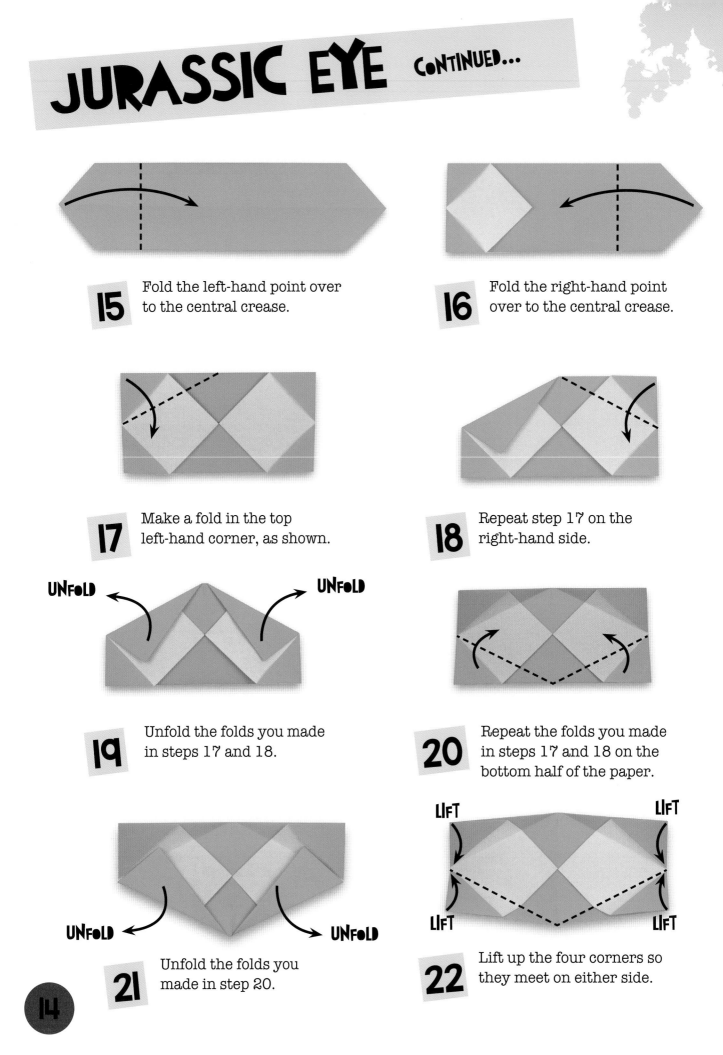

15 Fold the left-hand point over to the central crease.

16 Fold the right-hand point over to the central crease.

17 Make a fold in the top left-hand corner, as shown.

18 Repeat step 17 on the right-hand side.

UNFOLD   UNFOLD

19 Unfold the folds you made in steps 17 and 18.

20 Repeat the folds you made in steps 17 and 18 on the bottom half of the paper.

UNFOLD   UNFOLD

21 Unfold the folds you made in step 20.

LIFT   LIFT

LIFT   LIFT

22 Lift up the four corners so they meet on either side.

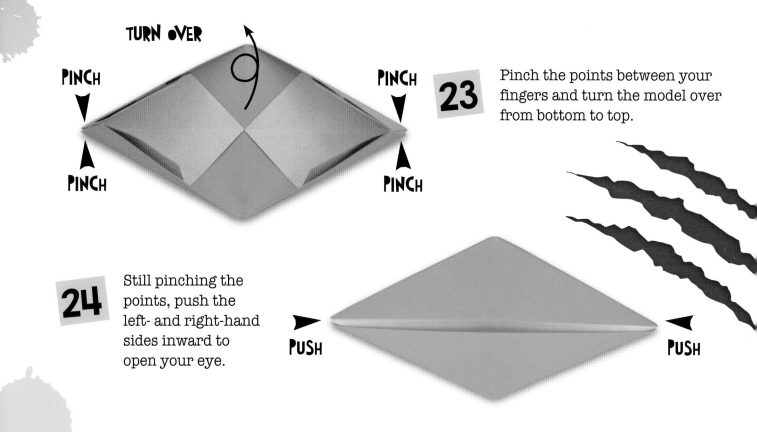

TURN OVER

PINCH

PINCH

PINCH

PINCH

23 Pinch the points between your fingers and turn the model over from bottom to top.

24 Still pinching the points, push the left- and right-hand sides inward to open your eye.

PUSH

PUSH

25 Draw the pupil of the eye in the middle of the white section. We don't know what dinosaur eyes really looked like, so you can pattern yours however you like.

26 Push and pull the eye to make it open and close.

FINISHED!

DINOSAUR EGG

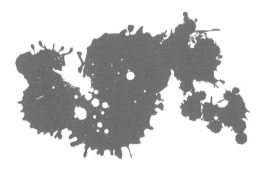

All dinosaurs started life as an egg. Why not make several eggs so you can have your very own dinosaur nest?

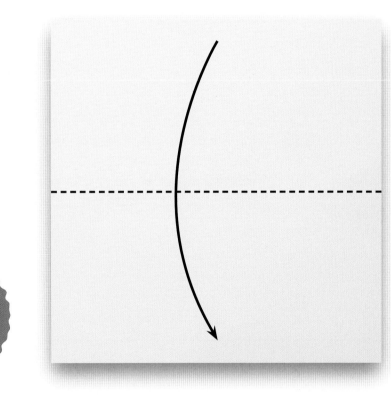

1

Place your paper like this, white side up, with a straight edge facing you. Fold in half from top to bottom.

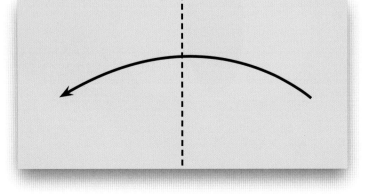

2

Fold the paper in half from right to left.

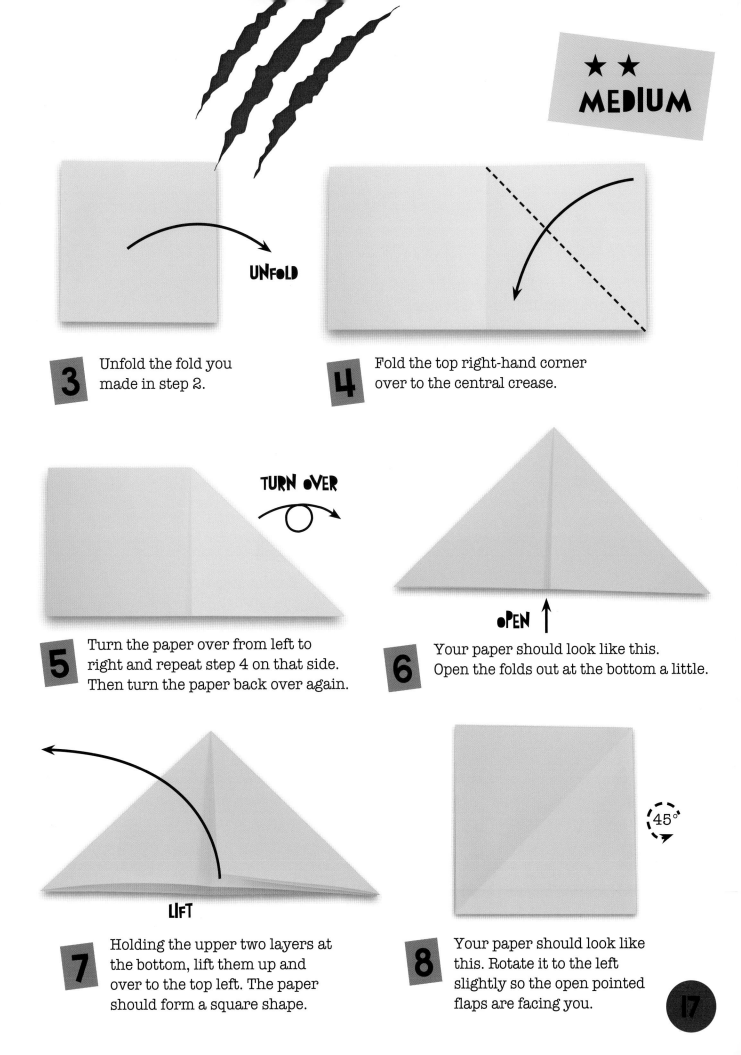

UNFOLD

3 Unfold the fold you made in step 2.

Fold the top right-hand corner over to the central crease.
4

TURN OVER

Turn the paper over from left to right and repeat step 4 on that side. Then turn the paper back over again.
5

OPEN ↑

Your paper should look like this. Open the folds out at the bottom a little.
6

LIFT

7 Holding the upper two layers at the bottom, lift them up and over to the top left. The paper should form a square shape.

45°

8 Your paper should look like this. Rotate it to the left slightly so the open pointed flaps are facing you.

17

9

Valley fold both layers of the right-hand point over as shown. The fold should be slightly slanted.

10

Repeat step 9 on the left-hand side.

11

Mountain fold the upper flap on both sides back behind the paper.

12

Make a small valley fold in the upper layer on the left-hand side, as shown.

13

Mountain fold the lower layer behind so it matches the fold from step 12.

14

Repeat steps 12 and 13 on the right-hand side.

15 Your paper should look like this. Rotate it 180°.

 180°

OPEN

16

Open out the paper at the top, and carefully push out all four sides.

17

And there's your egg, but where's the baby dino? It looks like it's already hatched and has scuttled away. Don't worry, you can catch up with it on the next page.

FINISHED!

BABY DINOSAUR

Now that you've made the eggs, it's time to fold a baby dinosaur or two. This is quite a simple project, but you'll need to make sure you crease your folds well.

1

Let's start by making a kite base. Place your paper like this, white side up with a corner facing you. Fold it in half from right to left.

2

Unfold the fold you made in step 1.

UNFOLD

3

Fold the left-hand point over to the central crease.

4

Fold the right-hand point over to the central crease.

5

Now that you've got a kite base, fold the left-hand point over to the central crease.

6

Fold the right-hand point over to the central crease.

7

Fold the paper in half from bottom to top.

q

Fold the bottom point of the top layer back up.

8

Fold the top points (both layers) down, as shown.

10 Fold the paper in half from left to right.

11 Your paper should look like this. Rotate it to the right so it matches the image in step 12.

90°

12 Valley fold the top left-hand point over, as shown.

13 Fold it the other way so it's also a mountain fold, then turn it into an inside reverse fold (see page 6). This is the head.

14 Fold the tip of the head over.

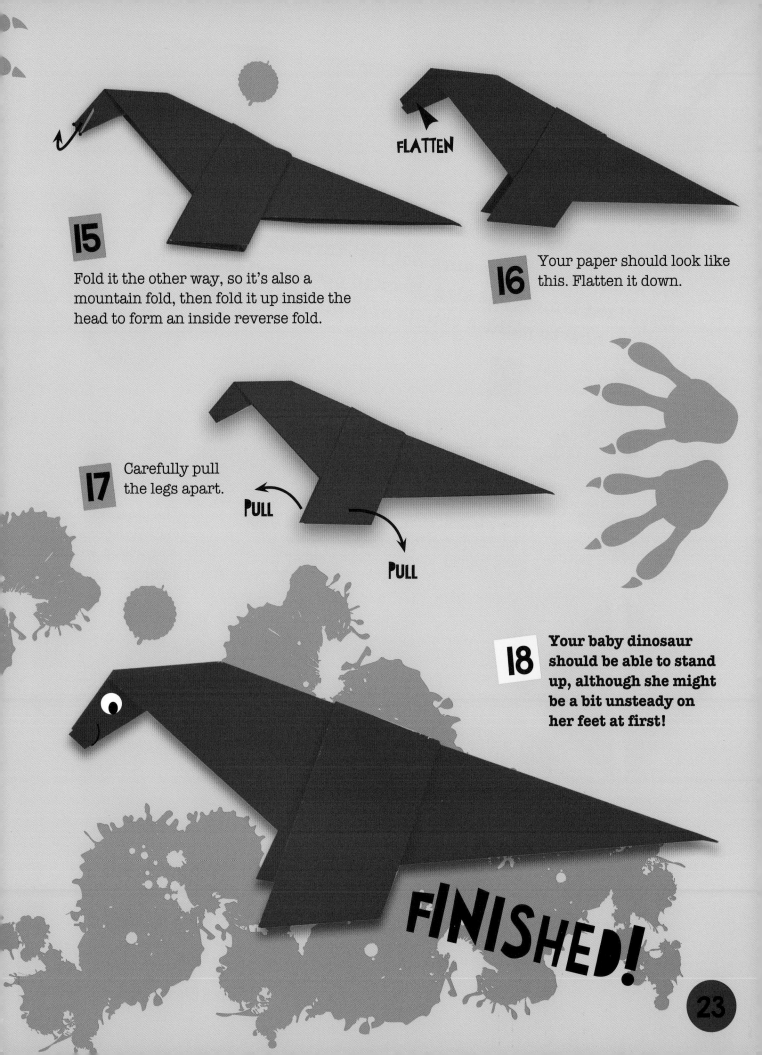

FLATTEN

15 Fold it the other way, so it's also a mountain fold, then fold it up inside the head to form an inside reverse fold.

16 Your paper should look like this. Flatten it down.

17 Carefully pull the legs apart.

PULL

PULL

18 Your baby dinosaur should be able to stand up, although she might be a bit unsteady on her feet at first!

FINISHED!

DINOSAUR FOOTPRINTS

We know about dinosaurs not just through their fossilized bones, but also through preserved footprints. Here's how to make a couple of giant dino steps.

1 Position your paper like this, white side down, with a corner facing you. Fold it in half from left to right, and unfold. Then fold it in half from top to bottom, and unfold.

2 Use your scissors to cut the paper in half along one of the crease lines, as shown.

3 Put the right-hand piece of paper to one side.

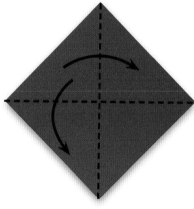

4 Turn the remaining piece of paper over from top to bottom.

TURN OVER

5 Fold the bottom point up and to the right so that the lower left edge lines up with the central crease.

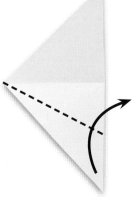

6 Repeat step 5 on the top point.

24

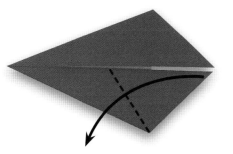

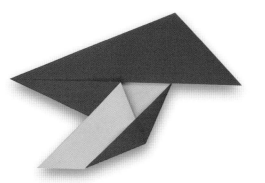

7 Lift the bottom-right point up and then down to the left.

8 Before you flatten the fold down, make a new fold on the bottom right-hand side, as shown, then flatten both folds down.

q Your paper should look like this. Repeat steps 7 and 8 at the top.

10 Get your other piece of paper and repeat steps 4 to 9.

FINISHED!

TURN OVER

11 Turn your pieces of paper over from top to bottom.

12 Position your models a step apart so they look like real footprints. Why not make some more for a dino that went on a long walk?

ARGENTINOSAURUS

Say "ar-jen-TEE-noh-SAW-rus"

This enormous, long-necked dino is one of the largest creatures ever to have lived on our planet. It was named after the country in which it was found—Argentina.

TAIL AND BACK LEGS

1 Start with your paper like this, white side up with a corner facing you. Valley fold it in half from top to bottom, and unfold. Then valley fold it in half from left to right, and unfold.

2 Fold the left- and right-hand points over to the central crease.

3 Fold the bottom point up to the top.

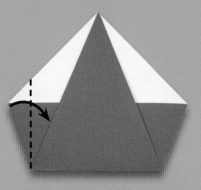

4 Fold the lower left edge across so it sits flush against the central triangle.

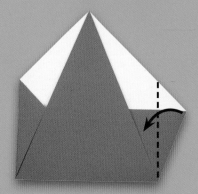

5 Repeat step 4 on the right-hand side.

26

UNFOLD

UNFOLD

UNFOLD

6 Unfold the folds you made in steps 3 to 5.

LIFT

7 Lift the central left point and move it down and to the right, as shown.

FLATTEN

8 Flatten the point down to form a triangle shape that goes over the central crease.

9 Your paper should look like this. Repeat steps 7 and 8 on the right-hand side.

10 Fold down the top point, as shown, so it lines up with the flaps made in steps 7 to 9.

11 Mountain fold the paper in half from right to left.

12 Your paper should look this. Put it to one side while you make the head and front legs.

27

1

Take your other piece of paper and repeat steps 1 to 9 from the tail and back legs section, so it looks like this. Now rotate the paper 180°.

180°

2

Mountain fold the paper in half from right to left.

3

Fold the top point down and to the left as shown.

4

Fold it the other way so it's also a mountain fold, then unfold.

5

Make a new fold at a slightly different angle, as shown.

6

Fold it the other way so it's also a mountain fold, then unfold.

7

PUSH

Push the top down so that the folds you made in steps 3 to 6 fold in on themselves, forming a step fold.

8

Flatten the paper down.

FLATTEN

9

Fold the top point over to the right, as shown.

10

Fold it the other way so it's also a mountain fold, then turn it into an outside reverse fold (see page 7). This is the head.

11

Your paper should look like this. Rotate it 90° to the right.

90°

12

Now bring back the first piece of paper and place it below the second one, like this.

13

Carefully push the second piece of paper so that the white triangle goes inside the first piece of paper while the legs go on the outside.

PUSH

14

Keep pushing until the two pieces of paper fit neatly together.

15

Lift it up carefully and your giant dino should be able to stand upright.

FINISHED!

GLOSSARY

eerie Strange and scary.

enormous Extremely large.

foreboding To give the impression that something bad is going to happen.

fossilize To preserve an animal or plant in a way that means it becomes a fossil.

Jurassic A prehistoric period during which the dinosaurs were alive.

preserve To keep something in its original state.

pupil The dark part of the eye that lets light through.

rotate To turn.

scuttle To move quickly.

FURTHER INFORMATION

BOOKS

George, Anna. *Origami Dinosaurs: Easy & Fun Paper-Folding Projects.* Minneapolis, MN: Super Sandcastle, 2017.

Harbo, Christopher. *Origami Palooza: Dragons, Turtles, Birds, and More!* North Mankato, MN: Capstone Press, 2015.

Montroll, John. *Origami Dinosaurs for Beginners.* Mineola, NY: Dover Publications, 2013.

Schultz, Walter-Alexandre. *Origami Dinosaurs.* New York, NY: Enslow Publishing, 2018.

WEBSITES

www.origami-make.org/howto-origami-dinosaur.php
Follow the instructions on this site to learn how to fold more dinosaurs.

www.origami-resource-center.com/origami-dinosaurs.html
This website offers instructions to make over 80 origami dinosaurs!

Publisher's note to educators and parents: Our editors have carefully reviewed these websites to ensure that they are suitable for students. Many websites change frequently, however, and we cannot guarantee that a site's future contents will continue to meet our high standards of quality and educational value. Be advised that students should be closely supervised whenever they access the Internet.

INDEX

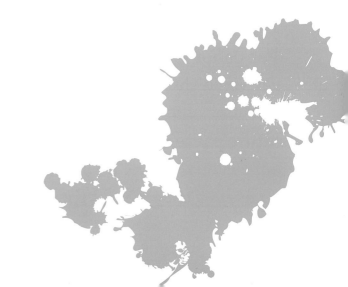